Then & Now
WELLS

F.C. Sampson Shoeing Forge seen here at No. 15 Union Street in 1910. Florence Sampson, William Francis Bertram Mogg (born 1907) and Amy Williams are outside the Sampson's family home. In 1914 Sampson and Jones were operating as motor engineers at No. 20 High Street and carriage builders in Portway. In 1932 Tinknells were trading as farriers from the same address.

Then & Now
WELLS

COMPILED BY CAROLINE BAGIAS

TEMPUS

Tempus Publishing Limited
The Mill, Brimscombe Port,
Stroud, Gloucestershire, GL5 2QG

ISBN 0 7524 2222 7

Typesetting and origination by
Tempus Publishing Limited
Printed in Great Britain by
Midway Colour Print, Wiltshire

VE Day celebrations in Queen Street in 1945. The second child in the front row is Maureen Brandon, former mayor. Her sister Pam Burridge (née Studley) is the fourth child in the same row. This view of Queen Street has changed very little.

CONTENTS

ACKNOWLEDGEMENTS

Many thanks go to all those who have helped me with photographs and information for the book, especially John and Audrey Sealy, Michael Baker and Jeffrey Allen for providing the main bulk of early photographs. Also George and Jack Paul, Mr and Mrs Allwright, Roger Cookman, Basil Mogg, Alan Woolley, Patrick Hopton, Michelle Machine, Sue Williams, Philip Welsh, Paul Fry, the late Des Glen, Lionel Browne and Graham Osborn, the Wells Museum Librarian.

William Trudgian, bootmaker is standing outside No. 1 Mill Lane around 1889. Mr Trudgian died at the age of forty-six leaving his wife Matilda to carry on the business. In 1902 she was known to be running the bootmakers shop at No. 3 Broad Street. In 1932 Nos 1-5 Broad Street was George and Son, K shoe agency. Today Basil Powell, the shoe shop, trades from the same premises.

PREFACE

Wells Then & Now represents the changes that have taken place in this city over the past 200 years. Here, Alan Woolley, a long time Wells' resident muses over what these changes may mean in the twenty-first century.

This is a book about the recent past of Wells. I am almost ninety years old, was born within twenty miles and have lived in sixteen parishes of Wells since 1936, when I turned up as the new, young doctor and country GP. I joined the Chamberlain Street Practice and helped run the Cottage Hospital for fifty years, so Caroline asked me for a few notes on changes affecting our lives.

Generally our standard of living has risen; there is no real poverty and we have access to a lot of gadgets unheard of fifty years ago. But change is not always to our benefit, there is often a price to pay.

Our society is consumed, among other things, by mobile phones and the Internet. Today a second-class letter can sometimes take anything from two to ten days to reach its destination. Although somewhat slower, compared to the pace of life in 1936, communication was extemely quick and reliable. I could write a letter to anywhere in the UK, post it by 4 p.m. and it would be delivered the next day at 7 a.m. A reply could be at my breakfast table fifteen hours from the time my letter was first sent. Postage cost 1_ pence. Very few people had telephones, so the quickest means of communication was the telegram; a message was wired out in morse code and sent to the nearest post office to the recipient. It cost 1s for twelve words and an extra 1d a word for longer messages, or if they wanted to pay for a reply, 2s. The message was delivered by hand by a telegraph boy in smart uniform on a red bicycle. He would then wait for a reply, which got back to the originator in the same way. It took about half an hour plus the cycle ride at each end; in most cases from town to town in no more than two hours, and the answer was written.

I had a car which would cost about £200 today, had a top speed of 40-50 mph, open five seater with canvas hood and took me approximately 6 hours to get 200 miles. There were empty roads, a lot of dust and not too many petrol stations. If I didn't want to drive to London or was in a hurry, I rang the Tucket Street Station at 7 a.m. to book a seat through to Paddington. The train left Wells at 8 a.m. and arrived in London at 10.30 a.m. I enjoyed a first-class breakfast on the way up and dinner on the way back. I can't remember the cost but I regarded it as very reasonable, and I was a lot worse off then than I have ever been since. So, the old days were really not all that bad!

Alan Woolley
April 2001

INTRODUCTION

Over the last 150 years photography has developed from the once crude process of image capture enjoyed by the few, into a simple method of recording enjoyed by the many. It has, in part, helped define the twentieth century and has grown into an influential and essential method of communication. It is important that we continue to document the images of today so that they will be here for tomorrow, and it is this importance that I have tried to highlight in this collection of photographs of Wells past and present.

In 1997 I opened Images photographic gallery in Wells to promote traditional monochrome photography, which stands the test of time and will therefore convey a dimension of how life is today. It is this essence that I have attempted to incorporate in *Wells Then & Now*. Many of the images included in this volume have not been published before and many will not have been seen outside private family situations.

The Cathedral keeps Wells alive with visitors from around the world all year long but it is to the ordinary men and women, who have made Wells what it is today, that I turn for the purposes of this book. Wells is fortunate in having records which go back to the thirteenth century, but books on the history of the city rather than the Cathedral itself are few. Until 1520 most properties were in institutional hands and after this time religious houses were dissolved and leases or freeholds were granted to courtiers, lawyers and officials. In 1638, 54% of properties in the city were in institutional ownership. The Liberty 90%, East Wells 40%. These estates remained intact until after 1830 and records identify properties by street. Names of streets in Wells have changed little and those which have are well known, such as Priston Row, now Priest Row, Grope Lane (then Grove Lane) now Union Street. Until the nineteenth century Chamberlain Street included Nos 1 to 9 New Street. Conversely, Portway ended at the junction with Wookey Hole Road. The lower section was variously attributed to Tucker Street, St Cuthberts or Beggar Street. In the 1870s street numbers and properties were usually identified by giving the side of the street and the nature of the two adjoining properties, who owned or occupied them, or both. The standard source of gauging population and wealth of areas was from a tax devised in the time of Henry VIII, known as The Lay Subsidy of 1524. The Hearth Tax of 1660-1700 is another useful source of local information. It gives the number of houses in an area; from which the population can be estimated. In the fourteenth century Wells had a population of 1,500 – the largest in Somerset. It almost equalled the total population of Bath and Taunton combined. The population has grown slowly but steadily since then whilst other surrounding places have grown relatively much faster. Today Wells is small compared with Bath's 80,000 or Taunton's 35,000.

Variety has always been a feature of Wells' mode of living; it has provided stability and prosperity for 800 years or more. The medieval core has changed little, however there have been fundamental architectural alterations probably incorporated when buildings were restored. Changes have taken place, new houses and roads have been built, buildings have been demolished, our memories fade and it is the photograph which reminds us of the past. This book, I hope, will be a fitting tribute to the history and the people of Wells.

S een here is an aerial view of Wells Cathedral and the Bishop's Palace beyond. The medieval city of Wells has long been recognised universally as a place of outstanding religious, architectural and historic importance. It has the largest concentration of listed buildings in Somerset. The Cathedral, cloisters, chapterhouse, Vicars' Close, Deanery and Bishop's Palace all make a unique and lovely city still almost as it was in the Middle Ages. Currently Wells itself is grossly under promoted, as compared with the Cathedral. It has much to be proud of and this should be more widely acknowledged.

Chapter 1
THE CATHEDRAL AND ANCILLARY BUILDINGS

WELLS CATHEDRAL

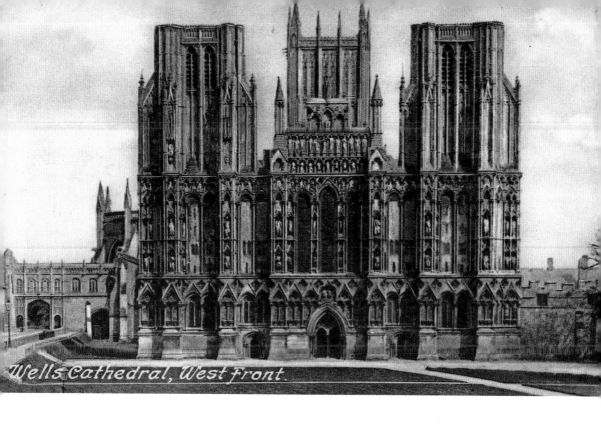

profusion of images and statues sculptured into niches, tabernacles and recesses, the canopies of which are supported by slender pillars of Purbeck marble. The construction of the present building commenced in 1180. It is built in the form of a cross with a square tower. The inverted strainer arches inside the Cathedral were added later.

The recent photograph shows the three tiers and Crowning Gable which make up the central pediment. In 1968 a new sculpture of Christ was added. The middle row shows the Apostles, and the third row the nine orders of angels. All are badly weathered, but behind them, their wings are still covered in the original crimson paint. Less understood is the purpose for the orifices above the angels. These may have acted as a microphone would today, conducting music from the inside of the Cathedral.

The West Front as seen here in the old photograph from around 1900, was built between 1220 and 1240 in pure English style and is thought to be one of the most superb pieces of Gothic architecture. It is adorned with a

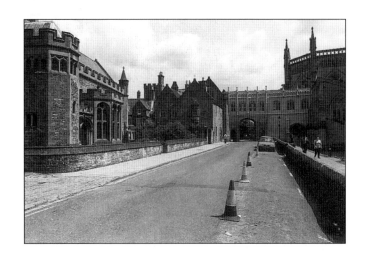

Enclosed within the Cathedral Green formerly free of civic and episcopal jurisdiction entirely under the discipline of dean and chapter are a number of noteworthy buildings – the deanery, museum and music school. The music school, seen to the left in the modern photograph, was previously the Theological College founded in 1840. Before this time the building was the old archdeaconry built in the time of Edward I. It was surrendered to the Crown in 1546, sold by Edward VI into lay ownership and later used as a brewery. In 1888 it was restored and used by the college as a library.

To the far right is the chapterhouse and before passing through the Chaingate, are the famous outside workings of the Cathedral clock with the quarterjacks. The early photograph dates from 1904.

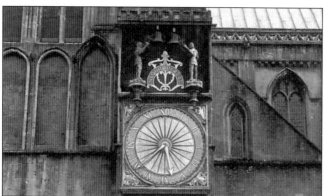

George and Harry Paul in 1959 with the quarterjacks during restoration. The Cathedral clock is dated to the second half of the fourteenth century and draws great crowds. It is not only a clock but essentially a model illustrating medieval concepts of creation and the universe. The clockface and two of the automata can be seen in the north trancept of the Cathedral. The quarters are struck by the seated figure known locally as Jack Blandiver. He kicks two bells with his heels while outside two figures in fifteenth century armour, four feet high and finely carved in oak, strike two bells with their axes. The motto on the face of the exterior clock translates as 'lest anything perish' which has appropriately been adopted by the Archaeological Society. From here one can pass through the Chaingate, built in 1459.

Workmen dismantling the iron railings in 1941. This, Bekynton's final gift to the Vicars Choral is yet another of the peculiar glories of Wells. It is really a bridge built over the roadway, devised by the Bishop to connect the chapterhouse stairway with the Vicars Close. Its excellence is in its simplicity. A covered walkway was needed so a bridge supported by three arches, one large for carts and two for foot passengers was built. It served as the main entrance to the city from the east and continued as such until Brown's Gate at the far end was closed. Recent restoration, paid for by the Friends of Wells, cost in excess of £30,000 and was completed in time for the Easter millennium celebrations. The physical fabric of this gateway has changed very little.

Vicars' Close seen here at the turn of the last century is a charming medieval street which survives in the modern world and looks much as it has done for the last five hundred years. Originally forty-two houses, twenty-one on each side, with a remarkable series of chimneys which were added in 1465. The Close was conceived as a college built round a quadrangle, having a chapel and library at its northern end. Built in perspective, the road gets narrower towards the far end. The distance between the rows of houses is sixty-five feet at the bottom end and fifty-six feet at the chapel end. The gardens were not part of the original design and the street consisted of cobble stones with a grass verge on either side. The only original gateway is that of No. 5. Number 16 has been converted to what appears to be a Georgian house, and No. 22 was restored to what is thought to be its original outward appearance.

The Vicars' chapel and Vicars' Close were built between 1407 and 1425 in an attempt to place the vicars under some form of discipline. Until the fourteenth century they had no common home. Documents suggest that the chapel had connections with the 'College of Chantry Priests' from its early days. The chapel was almost certainly a one storey building with a low roofed vestibule and was attached to No. 14, with an entrance set in the west wall. The present-day doorway was originally a window which was converted at a later date. The room above the chapel was built as a library at Bishop Bekynton's bequest. After many unsuccessful appeals, the vicars eventually entered into a lease with the Theological College.

4TH CENTURY CHAPEL, VICAR'S CLOSE, WELLS

Dean's Eye and more commonly as Brown's Gate after Richard Brown, a shoemaker who lived in the adjoining house in 1553. The road between Brown's Gate and the Chaingate was not always a closed thoroughfare. Before the reformation the clergy were seldom seen in public and the church, churchyard and deanery, like most ecclesiastical establishments, were surrounded by walls and gates. After the monastic character of the Cathedral had changed, the road through this area to the precinct soon became public. Several attempts were however made to close it. In 1841 it was proposed that the gateway be removed but the Chapter objected. Sixty years later, the Chapter again had Brown's Gate under consideration. Brown's Gate was eventually closed to traffic around the 1970s. The Gatehouse was converted in the 1930s to a comfortable hotel.

Tracing our steps back in the direction of the Cathedral Green we pass the crenallated gatehouse to the old deanery, once the second grandest ecclesiastic residence in Wells. It is an imposing heavily buttressed building which was used for seven hundred years. No dean has lived here since Dr Woodford's time. Nowadays it is used as the Diocesan's Offices.

This, the Bishop's third gateway, photographed during the early 1900s, has been known as Baron's Gate, the

On the two sides of the green, between Penniless Porch, seen on the right in 1914, and Brown's Gate at the north-west corner except for the gap in Sadler Street, houses have been built on both sides of the wall which remains for the most part. Those facing the market place with their Georgian and later frontages are still most picturesque. This, the southgate, leads us from the market place to the Cathedral Green once the main burial ground. It is so called because beggars would wait here seeking alms of church goers. It is an ornamental gateway, north of a row of twelve uniform houses. The penniless porch arch is of fine workmanship, groined and ornamented with rosettes. Bishops Bekynton's arms are curiously sculpted and his rebus – a name in a picture - can be seen as you walk from the green.

In the angle to the east of the inner exit a small blank oriel can also be seen. The rebus is made up of a flaming tar barrel on a pole, or a signal (a beck) in a barrel (a tun) 'Beck-in-tun'. The gateway has polygonal towers on the west archway with a four centred head decorated with fleurons-foliage in spandrels, shields and windows above. It is built in such a way that it seems to lead east but then turns north. The barriers have been removed but the porch remains much as it has always been.

Gatehouse and drawbridge were in working order as late as the 1930s when it was converted to a roadway. Before 1800 a figure-of-eight pond, known as the Horsepool lay between the Cathedral and the moat and gateway. This gateway has been photographed from inside the precinct wall. Some changes are not immediately noticeable; however, architectural elements such as the addition of battlements and alteration to the window casings become more obvious. Ivy has been removed, the centre statue is now missing and a small doorway has been added to the left bastion. The gas lamp between the arch has been replaced by a Victorian reproduction. Once a year the main gate is closed. This tradition demonstrates that the Bishop owns the freeway to the Palace.

Prior to the Bishop's Eye being built, access would probably have been through a low archway in the precinct wall; this would have allowed entrance from the Market Place to the palace gatehouse, drawbridge and moat. These fortifications were constructed in the 1300s. The drawbridge was only drawn once in 1831 when the Reform Act rioters destroyed the Bishop's Palace in Bristol. The moat was constructed by diverting the St Andrew's stream from the wells behind the Bishop's Palace. The

The Palace Gatehouse is seen in the old photograph from around 1904. To the tourist the Palace is chiefly famous for its wells and swans. The latter are a universal source of attraction owing to their habit of pulling a bell rope each day between three and four o'clock in the afternoon. This trick was taught over a hundred years ago to an old swan by a Victorian Bishop's daughter. This particular swan has been stuffed and can now be seen in the Wells Museum. His descendants carried on the tradition for many years. Recently a new pair have been introduced and trained. This view of the Cathedral from the front lawn of the Bishop's Palace has changed very little, apart from the ivy-clad buildings which the Victorians found attractive. The two bastions on either side of the drawbridge were once prisons for erring clerics and layfolk alike.

BISHOP'S PALACE, WELLS

It is here in the Bishop's Garden that the story of Wells began. Three springs produce more than 40 million gallons of water a day. The Palace, built around 1230, is set in a quadrangle surrounded by a wall. The moat outside the wall looks today much as it did when first built. It is one of the most interesting examples of castellated baronial mansions as well as of early domestic architecture. The ruins of the Great Chamber are now open to the sky and nothing but the walls remain. It was some 120ft by 70ft, lighted by nine windows with pointed arches, filled with tracery. Each wall angle was met by an octagonal turret and a staircase connecting with the roof. In the sixteenth century the timbers and roof lead were sold and more recently the south wall was removed leaving the site as we see it today. These days the Jocelyn building and chapel form the central section of the Palace.

The junction of Portway, Tucker Street and St Cuthbert Street is seen here in 1910. There has been a tradition in Wells which still continues today, to name streets after important and popular citizens. Sadler and Tucker were medieval mayors. Chamberlain was a local family name. Bekynton Avenue, Ken Close and Hervy Road all took their names from past Bishops. Balch Road is named after the Mendip cave explorer who also founded the museum and was curator for many years. Growth during the six centuries prior to 1886 made little impact to the size of Wells. The population in 1840 was 3,563 plus 313 in the Liberty. Even the arrival of the railways had little effect. In 1930, however, expansion into the surrounding countryside commenced

Chapter 2
STREETS AND
BUILDINGS

and has continued to such a degree that the medieval city is now engulfed in a mass of recent housing development. The entrance to the Priory Nurseries on the right no longer exists and the two houses to the far left of the photograph have been demolished.

WELLS CATHEDRAL FROM SHEPTON MALLETT ROAD.

The Shepton Mallet road into Wells in around 1920 was, until recently, the only entrance to the city from the south. The new bypass now carries the main bulk of traffic reducing city congestion. The public road in early times ran across the park meadow known today as the Palace Fields. This road was diverted when Bishop Jocelyn, (around 1206) obtained a licence from King John to enclose the park. Tor Street was created as part of this realignment. This seems to have been the last major adjustment to the town's road pattern for 600 years. The creation of the park has had continued impact on the city's form. Northward growth was hindered by the Mendips and to the south by the enclosed fields. As a result the town has tended to spread east to west rather than north to south. Tor Woods to the right of the photograph now belongs to the National Trust. The traveller who comes down Dinder Hill looks over a group of buildings which have no rival.

Penniless Porch, the Bishops Eye and conduit dominate the Market Place as seen in 1940. The twelve houses to the north were known as the New Works and would have been matched to the south, had Bishop Bekynton's death not intervened. Originally the market place was a roadway leading to the Cathedral and Palace with the high wall of the churchyard to the north and a canonical house to the south, behind which ran the roads, one across to Dulcot and the other along South Street and Southover. The front garden to the Archdeacon's house became part of the market place which accounts for its L-shape. There were once three buildings here. The High Cross, medieval conduit and the Exchequer, which was built to replace the Guildhall in the Rubwith Almshouse. The Market House, to the right of the Bishop's Eye is now the Crown post office built on the site of the Palace Mill.

E MARKET SQUARE, WELLS.

The Crown Hotel (top) probably photographed sometime after the war, is the most imposing building on the south side of the market place. It is from here that the Quaker leader William Penn preached in 1692 from the window above the Penn Bar which was then the Royal Oak. The hotel resulted from the uniting of three terraced houses dating from 1450. Successive owners have preserved the authenticity of the interior. It has fine oak windows at the rear overlooking the courtyard, and to the front a good view of the market place and south-west aspect of the Cathedral. Numbers 8 and 10, once the famous Phillip's Photographic Studio, now form part of the hotel complex. A house east of No. 10 was demolished in 1839 and in 1952 the Wells City Council proposed to demolish Nos 8 and 10 in order to open up views of the restored Crown.

Tom Price (below) was publican from 1912 to 1954, one of the longest serving licensees in Wells. Freddy Chapman took over from him when he retired. Sidney and Barbara Price became landlords of the New Inn in St Thomas Street, thereby continuing the family involvement in the licencing trade until 1989. The Crown was commandered during both the First and Second World Wars. Some of the upstairs rooms were used to make and assemble aircraft parts, and troops were billeted here. At this time bed and breakfast cost 6s a night, early morning tea was 3d for a cup or 6d for a pot. Cold lunch was 2s, hot lunch 2s 6d, and a four-course dinner was 3s. In 1993 The Crown was under receivership.

Together with Peter Ayton, the current proprietor Adrian Lawrence set about improving The Crown's fortunes. The hotel is run as an inn offering traditional hospitality.

Forms of transport have come a long way from the days of the horse and cart. In 1835 the corporation acquired the Palace Mill and the present Market Hall was then built. It was originally a colonnaded building having been adapted around 1903 to its present day appearance. It became The Crown post office in 1923. In January 2000 a proposal was made by the Market Hall Trust, followed in March by a poll and a public display in the town hall. This proposal for use as a post office counter, tourist information and exhibition space was turned down by the council and since then the building has continued to stand empty. Hopefully a viable solution will be found in time and enable this prominent building to be put to proper use.

The photograph below from 1927 shows members of the Wells fire brigade standing in front of the engine house in the market place. The local fire brigade was established in 1874 and played an essential part in all special occasions and processions, including the carnival. Initially they would have participated with horse-drawn vehicles which were stabled in the undercroft of the Exchequer. In 1937 the fire station relocated to Princes Road to a site previously occupied by a garage. In 1991 this fire station was demolished to make way for Tesco supermarket. The new station has been built alongside the westerly bypass. Today the brigade offers a twenty-four hour, round the clock service. The recent photograph shows from left to right: Firefighter Pickford,

Sub Officer Bowley, Firefighter Holmes and Leading Firefighter Sheppey standing behind their fire engine during the recent millennium celebrations on the Cathedral Green.

DECLARING THE POLL.
WELLS 1910
SANDYS. 6164.
SILCOCK. 4841.
NO.7.
PHILLI

Election day 1910 when the results were announced from the Town Hall. This building with its Law Courts and gaol was erected in 1778 on the site of a Canonical house. It replaced the former Market Hall and Exchequer at the centre of the market place. The porch and arcade were added in 1861, the balcony and round windows in 1933. The Assize Court last sat here in 1970. The council chamber and Parkes Room were opened in 1998 and a licence for the conduct of civil marriages given. The main hall is one of the finest public rooms in Somerset and can accomodate 180 guests. The purchase and building of the Town Hall was authorised by an act of parliament made during the reign of George III. A point of interest is that until 1988 the Town Hall rates were £8 a year because Wells had a special dispensation made under the same act. The local Finance Act in 1988 ended this and the rate rose to £5,220.

S adeler Street is shown below around 1949. It was written this way in the fifteenth century and was probably named after John Sadeler a former MP and mayor for Wells. Before the 1700s public houses included The Swan, Fleur de Luc, Harts Head, the Mitre and White Horse. At No. 3 Sadler Street, Pavey the tobacconist stocked a range which included Dunhill, Havana and Jamaican cigars. The Old Priory tearoom offered afternoon teas, lunches and morning coffee, homemade bread and cakes and a shop downstairs. Wicks, one of the oldest firms supplied house furnishings, where everything from bedding to floor coverings was available. T. Wicks and Sons, now Allen Harris, were auctioneers and estate agents for the Halifax Building Society.

To the east side of the street was Vowles the chemist and the Midland Bank which has now become the HSBC. Having widened the road around the 1930s the city council is about to complete the job of narrowing it again.

The Swan Hotel is situated to the west side of Sadler Street which runs north from the High Street. First reference in city records were made in 1422. It was largely rebuilt in the sixteenth century, flooded in the eighteenth century and extensively altered over the succeeding years. It was the main coach and posting house during the Turnpike era and later with the arrival of the railway ran its own Swan Bus, a four-in-hand. In 1955 it was described as a fifteenth-century hotel, having three lounges, central heating, hot and cold running water and garaging for thirty-five cars. The early photograph shows the main facade much as it is today apart from the double-arched entrance probably adapted around 1900. The present owner Christopher Chapman has recently acquired the Star Hotel in the High Street. This hotel with its ten bedrooms will be amalgamated once more with The Swan; £250,000 has been suggested as the figure needed to raise it to a three-star rating in line with that of The Swan. In 1769 The Swan was leased to Charles Tudway and later purchased by his son, Clement in 1798. It remained in the family until 1885 when it was sold to Louisa George.

The High Street (below) in around 1932. W.H. Harrill at No. 42 was a butchers shop. Next door was Holloway and Sons Haircutting Salon. The City Café, Kings Head, Sampsons and The Star Hotel are seen further up on the north side of the street. Opposite are Barnes, Hallidays, Davys and the Central Hotel. Some 800 years ago the main street was called Cheap Street. A row of stalls or shambles extended from The Star Hotel to Broad Street. Wells has many public houses and hotels today. In 1840 there was a total of 29 Inns and Hotels listed in the city. To name but a few that were in the High Street: The George at No. 7, The King Charles Parlour at No. 8, the Katheryn Whele, later Wickenden's Confectioners at No. 11 and the Christopher at No. 35. In 1862 the latter premises were home to the

Somerset Hotel which then became Halliday's Antique shop. It was from here that Queen Mary acquired the pieces for her famous doll's house. Many longstanding businesses have ceased trading. Amongst those that remain are Nowell's Antiques and Wicks in the market place, Whitings at No. 68 High Street and Spencers in Tucker Street.

In 1830 improvements were made to the main approaches to the town. To the south, Wet Lane which was 12ft wide at its narrowest point was widened to become Broad Street, as seen in this old postcard from 1948. Its alignment was continued across the former priory gardens making Priory Road the new approach from Glastonbury. At one time there was a cross at the junction of Queen Street and St John's Street. The most interesting aspect of the early postcard is the lack of shop windows, signs and vehicles, although the buildings have changed very little. Sampson's garage, to the right, survived until the mid-1980s. Borthwick and Co. have ceased trading whilst the Silver Studio has moved here from Sadler Street. Today it is as the sign suggests, a one-way street, traffic having previously taken this route through town via Sadler Street to Bath and Bristol.

Priory Road as seen in 1904 was built in 1836 and is named after a religious settlement dedicated to St John the Baptist, through the grounds of which it now runs. It is presently the main road to Glastonbury. Previously the exit road was via St John's Street and Southover. The main route at this time ran down the High Street, turning left into Queen Street at the City Arms with its rounded corner which enabled the stagecoaches to take it at speed. In 1840 the buildings opposite the sub-post office were once occupied by the Antelope Hotel. THe year 1974 saw the opening of the Good Earth health food shop and later the restaurant, a radical move at the time. There were two cinemas, three garages and the main Bus Station all at one time in Priory Road. In the early picture the trees are well attended and to the far right is the old Palace Theatre which has only recently been demolished.

Troops with their lorries are seen above during the First World War as they are about to leave Princes Road to move off for the front. To the far right beyond the army lorries is the octagonal market house, long since gone, and the Victorian houses in Market Street. The recent photograph shows the St John Ambulance hut. After seventy years here they are to move to new quarters adjacent to the Leisure Centre at Portway. Part of the proposed development of this area involves the closure of Princes Road, in order to allow the road to be used for buses. The new transport interchange building is to include a waiting area with combined ticket office, information and refreshment kiosk. New toilets, already underway have been designed to minimise maintenance costs.

An A.C.T. Jewell charabanc, below, is parked outside the Railway Tavern in Southover on a day out. This photograph was taken around 1920; Reg Stevens (Snr) is the driver. This ale house was first known as the Travellers Rest on account of its providing lodgings for 'gentlemen of the road'. It later upgraded to the Railway Tavern and in 1861 it became the Railway Family Hotel and Commercial Inn run by John Buck. The original Victorian bus canopy can be seen alongside The Crown Hotel in the market place. A bus station was built in Priory Road next to the Regal cinema. This became a DIY shop when part of the Princes Road car park was later designated for use by buses and coaches. It is now a

furnishing centre. To the right in the recent picture is the existing ticket office with St Cuthbert's church in the background. A number 377 bus is seen here leaving for Yeovil.

Princes Road car park was once the cattle market, as seen here around 1941. The old photograph shows sheep pens in the background behind the assembled crowd who look as though they are dressed in their Sunday best. Cllr Wheeler is seen here taking charge of the Farmers' Red Cross sale which raised funds for the war effort. Markets were held weekly on a Saturday whilst a cattle market was held in Market Street on the first Saturday in the month. Plans for the first phase of the Princes Road development have begun. The sale of the site was still pending at the time of publication. There have been warnings that this could lead to the demise of the city centre. This aerial view from St Cuthbert's church tower may remind people in the future how things used to be, should the proposed development take place.

Apart from the cars parked along the left side of the road St Cuthbert's Street has not altered significantly. Some of the properties which were once small shops have now become residential. Until 1856 it was appropriately named after the patron of Wells' only church. Traffic used to flow from the High Street and but now flows one-way towards the church. The nearest shop on the north side of the street was once Stevens' sweetshop, where brown paper bags, string and stationery could be purchased, and further up on the same side of the road was Miss Morgan's shop, which sold crockery and household goods – and even repaired umbrellas! Number 2 was W.H. Paul builders and decorators, now the Lighthouse Bookshop. Today Leon's at No. 57 is a barbers. His is a long established business where customers

are known to travel from as far as Bath and Bristol. Cook's newsagents at No. 31 is a family business which has seen three generations. Sometime during the mid-twentieth century some of the shop numbers in this street changed.

Tucker Street, seen in the above photograph, in 1904, owes its name to the woolcombers or 'tuckers' who in medieval times had their quarters here. It is certain that Wells was noted for its cloth industry. The only resident in Tucker Street 600 years ago was Walter Towker. He was an MP and mayor in 1459. There are two well-known public houses, the Mermaid and the Cheddar Valley. The former was a sixteenth-century tavern whilst the Cheddar Valley acquired its name from the railway line which was used in the transportation of strawberries grown in the Cheddar Valley. On May Day, on account of the cattle market and auction ring, this area was a hive of activity attracting a good number of gypsies selling horses. The pubs stayed open until 4 p.m. before which time fighting would have broken out in front of the Mermaid and was a common occurence which attracted huge crowds. The street is mainly residential today. Davis Terrace to the far right is joined by new houses and the entrance to Tesco supermarket.

The majority of those who visited Wells as a holiday centre would have arrived by rail; London was 121 miles away. In 1908 a first-class return ticket to Paddington was 40s and second-class 27s. The railway arrived late in Wells. First was the joint Somerset and Dorset line followed by the East Somerset line in 1862. On 3 March 1859 the official opening of the railway took place. A procession led by the mayor and council greeted the directors and officers of the railway company. When the train carrying the directors entered the borough a royal salute was fired from the Russian gun. The procession returned to the Town Hall, where a selection of music was played throughout the afternoon and evening. The Bristol and Exeter line finally reached Wells in 1870 terminating at Tucker Street station.

Eight years later a level crossing was built near to the Sherston Inn. With the reorganisation of the railways in the 1960s and after only 100 years, Tucker Street station and the remaining railway network finally ceased, terminating the history of the railway in Wells.

RTWAY, WELLS

Wookey' as it was locally known. It actually began from the bottom of St Cuthbert's Street joining the Wookey road at the brow of the hill. Wells' cemetery is located here having been consecrated in 1855. Since the opening of the new bypass the main routes to Cheddar and Wookey Hole follow the old Cheddar Valley line and Whitings Way, a new road which meets the northern stretch of the bypass. The most obvious difference between the two photographs are the houses to the right in Portway. The large house seen to the far right of the early photograph is still there although it is obscured by the houses in the later photograph. To the left is Jubilee Terrace from where Willmott Transport first operated, and further up are the old Wheelwright cottages.

Portway in around 1900 seems to have come to an end at the junction with Wookey Hole Road. The lower portion was variously attributed to Tucker Street, St Cuthbert's, Beggar Street or just 'the way towards

The lower end of Portway Road can no longer be accessed, except by pedestrians. In the short time since these photographs have been taken a crossing has been constructed and the access appropriately altered. On the night of 18 June 1926 there was a terrific storm. As Wells is in a valley the obvious consequence was severe flooding, with water sweeping down from the Mendips. It took its natural course down Sadler Street and the High Street. The water dammed off Chamberlain Street but played havoc elsewhere going into shops and homes. When it was over there was a united attempt at cleaning it all up. When newly arrived visitors turned up for their usual sightseeing they had no idea there had been a storm because it had been so localised. Both photographs show the Portway annex, previously the Girls' Blue School, with telephone kiosk at the point where Lovers Walk meets lower Portway. This was, until recently the main road to Cheddar and Wookey.

St Mary's Convent, Wells.

0 1856 B

S t Mary's Convent seen in the old photograph in 1914, is now the Elim Pentecostal church. The Mendip Christian Fellowship also meet here, as do the Christadelphians. Chamberlain Street was until the end of the nineteenth century regarded as 'running-up to The Liberty' and the lower end was known as Beggar Street. Opposite the Bubwith Almshouses was the Byre Theatre once home to the Mendip Players. The most imposing building is No. 11 the former Carmelite convent, The Vista. This description alluded to the cleared area facing the mansion, however, the name has now become attached to the house itself. It seems to have been the usual residence of the leading non-ecclesiastical inhabitant of Wells until the Tudways used their wealth to build the Cedars. The Roman Catholic church which adjoins the Vista was completed in 1889 and Nos 8–12, the houses at the top end of the street, were built over a period of fifty years. Nos 2 and 4 were later known as the King's Arms and The Angel.

Melborne House at No. 20 Chamberlain Street photographed around 1930. At this time the practice was run by Drs Allen and Hinks who held their surgeries here whilst Dr Mullins was at No. 2 New Street, the house at the corner of the Liberty which is appropriately named after him. The other doctor also practising in Chamberlain Street was Dr Manning who lived across the road next to The Limes, so called because of the row of lime trees which once stood near these houses. In 1936 Dr Alan Woolley joined the Melborne practice and in 1938 Tom Melrose joined Dr Manning. He was replaced by Dr Pinching after the war. This practice relocated to the Presbytary, more recently used as a kindergarten affiliated to the Roman Catholic school.

A GP's pay at this time was £800 per annum, with a joining fee of 11s to the BMA. The beautiful gardens at the back of Melborne House are long gone and have been replaced by the Melborne House Mews.

New Street is seen here in the old photograph from 1910. There was no extensive development before the Planning Act of 1947 so ribbon development was avoided in Wells and the city still retains two superb entrances, one from Bristol and one from Shepton Mallet, and green fields run right up to the old buildings in Wells. In 1830 the complex set of junctions at the top of New Street were rationalised and directed towards New Street away from the steep and tortuous Old Bristol Road. The new northern bypass, the A39, includes Mountery Close. Ritchie House is seen here to the right in both photographs. From around the mid-1920s up to just before the war this was home to the Girls' High School, established in 1888 in the Market Place. Before it moved to New Street in 1927 the school was sited above the West Cloister. It was purchased in 1948 by the Cathedral School who then used it as a junior boys' house. The Prudential Garage to the left has now been demolished. Before the road at the top end of Sadler Street was widened the corner was occupied by St Helen's Cross and the precinct wall lacked battlements.

The earlier image shows a view of Wells Cathedral from the Liberty around 1900. These new canons' houses were described as 'the most beautiful buildings in Wells'! The wonderful orchards and gardens seen here no longer exist. The precincts which surround the Cathedral are known as the Liberty. Bishop Jocelyn created it in 1207, as this area was free from city law. The name is perpetuated in the two streets which run at right angles; The North and East Liberties where canons and school boys lived alongside one another. The Old Canons Barn is opposite on the north side. Further along at No. 7 is St Andrews Lodge, the original Boys' Blue School. At the corner on the site of the first song school and former College of St Ann is the Georgian house known as the Cedars, the principal Cathedral School building. Adjacent and to the right of the Cedars is the 'De Salis'. On the corner with the Liberty is the house where Dr Claver Morris lived; he is well-known for his diaries which give an important insight into aspects of eighteenth century life. Several prebendary houses in the East Liberty now form part of the Cathedral school complex.

The old image shows St Thomas Street in 1936. It is the eastern continuation of St Andrew's Street previously known as East Wells, and By-est-Walls. It was a very poor area ridden with disease. Unlicenced ale houses abounded and employment was casual. Being part of the out-parish of St Cuthbert's it had no church of its own until the mid-nineteenth century. Consecration of St Thomas' church took place on the Feast of St Thomas and Dean Jenkyn's birthday thus explaining the choice of dedication. It has always been the main road out of Wells to London and in 1930 the corner house at the junction of the East Liberty and St Andrews Street was demolished to widen the road. Tor Street is to the left of the photograph and leads to Shepton Mallet. Towards the end of the nineteenth century public houses such as The Fountain, The Goat (at No. 8 seen to the far left of the early photograph), The Lamb (at No. 25 seen in the recent photograph to the near right, with its bowed window) and The New Inn at No. 60 existed. In 1891 at the height of the Temperance movement a coffee tavern and reading room was established at No. 7 St Thomas' Street is now mainly residential.

The laying of the Foundation Stone for the Cottage Hospital is taking place here in 1929. In medieval times a hospital was a charitable institution sometimes providing schooling or care for the elderly or infirm. The Priory of St John was the first hospital in Wells. During the early part of the nineteenth century increasing wealth in the country was for the first time directed on a national scale towards providing education, improving and regulating factories and helping those in the community who were destitute through no fault of their own. Hospitals were built for the sick and mentally ill. Churches such as St Thomas, the Roman Catholic church, the Baptist chapel, Methodist chapel and a number of mission and reading rooms, together

Chapter 3
HEALTH AND
SOCIAL WELFARE

with a strong Temperance Movement were established in Wells. St Thomas' School, the Central School and other educational estabishments continued this progress with the Church as always being the pioneer of education.

THE
OUNDATION STONE

Patients and Friends at the annual
Tea Party of Priory Hospital.

Patients and friends are seen here at the Annual Tea Party of the Priory Hospital in 1966 where Mrs D.A. Cox the organiser cuts the cake. Standing behind her is Cllr Campkin and Mr Woods the chairman of the Friends. Provision for the poor in the eighteenth century was less compassionate. The Priory Hospital on the Glastonbury Road was built in 1837 on land purchased from Robert Charles Tudway. The four acres, three rods and nineteen perches required cost £850. The Wells Union Workhouse, as it was known then, catered mainly for the poor and under-privilaged children. In the 1860s this concept had changed to caring for the infirm and elderly poor folk. In 1948 the National Health Service upgraded and renamed the hospital the Wells Infirmary. Latterly there were four wards providing a total of sixty-nine beds. A day hospital, physiotherapy and occupational therapy unit were available to both in and out patients. Modernisation over the last 40 years resulted in a hospital which provided treatment and care for the elderly. Plans have now been approved to develop Priory Hospital as a Primary Care Centre along with the health centre.

The county lunatic asylum near Wells, opened in 1848, was originally intended to accommodate 300 patients. Further buildings were added over the years and in 1950 there were 1,000 patients. Dr Boyd the first Superintendent quickly instituted a curative programme. Many pioneering treatments of mental illness were carried out. In 1957 out of 631 admissions 70.6% were discharged within three months. In spite of the difficulties created by shortages in staff, accommdation and finance, the Mendip Hospital continued to be closely involved with the local community for 150 years. It was a place to which those in mental distress could turn and stood as a living testimony of humanity. It finally closed in 1990. The recent photograph

shows work in progress on the chapel's tower and spire. All these buildings have now been adapted for residential use.

The Wells and District Hospital seen here in 1904, and known locally as the Cottage Hospital, was founded in 1874 by Lord Arthur Harvey, Bishop of Bath and Wells. Originally it was two cottages on the same site at the top of St Thomas Street. It contained six beds and was supported by voluntary contributions. It was rebuilt in 1895 with funds left by E.M. Plumptree, Dean of Wells (1881-91). Additions were made in 1929 and 1979. There were three wards; a general male, general female and maternity. Over the years the services provided have varied. They have included general medical and surgical, maternity, geriatric and casualty. There have never been more than about forty beds in total, and sadly at the time of publication the ward on the ground floor is not in use. The hospital today mainly takes in elderly patients and continues to provide excellent accident and emergency and consultancy services.

At the time of the photograph, below, in 1904 the men's ward was on the first floor. It later became the female ward and the men's ward was transferred to the ground level. There were also a number of single rooms used for seriously ill patients. In 1936 there was one maternity bed. Most women delivered their babies at home and cases for admission were only made in grave emergencies. After the war there were ten maternity beds whilst the Orange Grove in Ash Lane provided about six beds for those who preferred to have their babies in more private and comfortable surroundings. Although this was a private unit it was easily affordable and was run by a Sister Johnson. Since that time women have

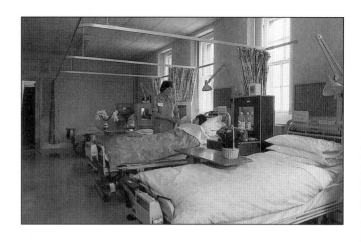

continued to have their babies in hospital. Today, it is possible that many women given the choice would prefer the comfort of their own home to the clinical surroundings of a hospital.

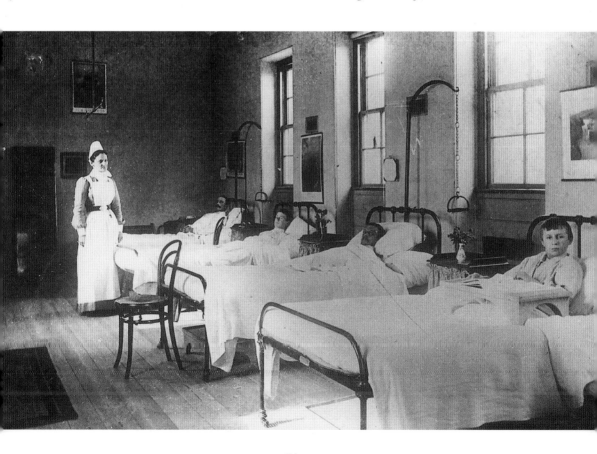

Dr Alan Woolley in 1950 on horseback at Sharcombe House, Dinder. On occasions when the weather was bad house calls were sometimes made this way. Dr Woolley came to Wells in 1936 having worked as a house surgeon at the Bristol Royal Infirmary. Now retired and in his late eighties, he has played a major role in the community for the best part of the last sixty years. Dr Allen the senior partner at Melborne House died unexpectedly during the war and Dr Woolley subsequently became head of the firm from 1948 to 1986 when he was replaced by Dr Ashman. When the consultants visited the Cottage Hospital the local doctors were expected to administer anaesthetics and assist with operations when required. Between 1946 and 1970 there were approximately 100 T/As (tonsil and adenoid) performed a year. Dr Woolley only remembers having to perform four caesareans in the course of a twenty-year period.

The St John Ambulance members in the old photograph are seen on Armistice Day 1954. The recent photograph shows today's members with the new ambulance, a gift from the Freemasons. It was dedicated in July and the key handed to the Divisional Superintendent Gerard Woods. From left to right: Kevin Matthews, Lisa Woods, Robert Earney, Pauline Pickford, Les Collins, Derek Armer, Gerard Woods, Jason Nuttycombe, Alex Fowler, Diane Brown, Philippa Tungate. The Wells Division was formed in 1930. The Order of St John, the parent organisation, has existed for almost 900 years. The movement is one of many that works free of cost to and for the community. There was little organised first-aid in 1905 when the first official ambulance known as 'The Litter' was handed over. In 1935 a second-hand billiard hall became the first and

only St John Ambulance Headquarters and was erected in the corner of the old cattle market. In 1948 there were forty voluntary maintained and manned ambulances of which eighteen were run by the brigade and eleven by the British Red Cross. New Headquarters are to be built adjacent to the leisure centre.

R esidents wait in front of the Llewellyn Almshouses, Priest Row in 1958, before going on a day out. Cllr and Mrs Mogg are in the centre with Mrs Melrose the doctor's wife between them. It was commonplace in the past for well-known citizens to leave bequests. Amongst these were Bishops Bubwith, Stills and Willes and former mayors, Llewellyn and Harper. The Bubwith Almshouses in Chamberlain Strret were built in 1436, north of St Cuthbert's church and were paid for from the legacy of Bishop Bubwith. Further bequests followed from Bishop Still and Bishop Willes. All told the almshouses housed thirty-four poor men and women. Henry Llewellyn, a seventeenth-century mayor, left a bequest for the almshouses to be built in 1615 on the east side of Priest Row. They were rebuilt in the 1880s on an enlarged site, incorporating several neighbouring houses. Provision was made for ten elderly women to each have a parlour, bed room and a small garden. Archibald Harper, mayor in 1702 left a house in Chamberlain Street.

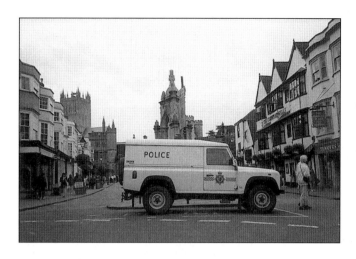

Below are the special Somerset Constabulary during the standing-down of the wartime organisation in 1945. In 1568 under the Charter of Elizabeth I the corporation were authorised to have a gaol in the city. Before this time the Bishops had held powers to hold courts for the trial of criminals as well as for civic cases. The cellars of the City Arms were once the gaol. They continued as such until about 1800 after which time it transferred to the Town Hall. The cells here are used now for prisoners awaiting trial in the magistrates court. Today police presence is minimal and the call for 'bobbies on the beat' is stronger than ever. In 1846 the duty of the police sergeant was to be firm and just, and at the same time kind and conciliatory. Public houses were allowed to open on Sundays, Christmas Day and Good Friday to receive travellers, but alcohol was forbidden. The punishment for not paying a fine was six hours in the stocks. Absence of crime was seen to be the best proof of the police force's efficiency.

GRAND PAROCHIAL BAZAAR,

ST. CUTHBERT'S, WELLS,

Parish Magazine.

SOUTH EAST VIEW OF St CUTHBERTS CHURCH WELLS

FEBRUARY, 1924.

Tuesday & Wednesday, Feb. 26 & 27

became Dean in 1845 he found a growing slum area to the east of the city. He had planned to have a church built but died before accomplishing the task. His wishes were finally fulfilled when the foundation stone to St Thomas' church was laid. The architect in 1856 was S.S. Teulon who has now come to be recognised as an important Victorian architect.

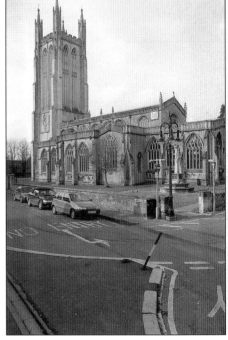

St Cuthbert's church was built by Cathedral masons and its priests were usually provided by the Chapter. The only surprise in Wells is that there were no other churches except chantry chapels until the building of St Thoma's. The present building has its origins in the thirteenth century. The central tower collapsed in 1561 and was replaced by the grand 122ft high tower which tourists today often mistake for the Cathedral. When Richard Jenkyn

Both the Cedars and St Andrew's Lodge, seen here, are used by the Cathedral School today. The Cedars was once the family home to the Tudways and St Andrews was the first Boys' Blue School. In 909 Wells became the seat of a Bishop. This meant worship for which music played a fundamental part. The first Song School was thus established. In 1229 a grant was given for houses and land in Mounterye. This name corresponds to the present North Liberty. These houses were later converted into the College of St Ann. The school relocated temporarily and in 1480 the school room in the West Cloister was brought into use and occupied until 1870. In 1609 William Evans bought the former college. His family owned this house until it was bought by Charles Tudway in 1755 who later built the Cedars. This Georgian house was used as a Military Hospital during the war and later by the Theological College. In 1926 it was leased to the Cathedral School. Finally in 1965 the Dean and Chapter persuaded the Church Commissioners to buy the estate which they now lease to the school. The school became co-educational in 1969.

The Girls' Blue School, Portway Annex, at the turn of the last century. The United Charity School was founded in 1641 at the Bubwith Almshouses. In 1713 St Andrews was built in the Liberty with the prime objective of educating the poorest children. Further rooms were added in 1815 when the Cathedral School united with the Blue School under one Headmaster. This amalgamation lasted until around 1825 when the school relocated to Soho House at the lower end of Chamberlain Street. The two stone slabs inscribed with the Duke of Monmouth's motto can be found in the wall outside Milton at the Blue School. The School House was replaced around 1911 by the building now used by The Wells Operatic Society. The Portway Annex as it has come to be known locally was the girls' school. In 1962 the Wells County School was opened alongside that of the Secondary Modern School. In 1970 the two schools amalgamated to form a fully comprehensive school. The recent photograph shows the entrance to the new Sports Development Centre at the Blue School specially built to mark the year 2000.

Pupils from the Central School are seen around the 1950s in the old photograph. The school off St Johns Street was built in the mid-nineteenth century. The original Hospital of St John was founded in 1220 by Bishop Jocelyn on the site of what was the Central School. The foundation had a Chantry Chapel and its own cemetery which lay beneath the school grounds. It was, however, dissolved in 1539. The main range of buildings survived until 1858 when the site was cleared to make way for the new school. Peter Sherston conveyed part of the ancient Priory of St John to the Bishop of Bath and Wells in trust for the erection of two Church of England schoolrooms, one for boys and the other for girls. The rooms were 60ft long and 20ft wide to cater for 200-300 pupils. The old school has now been

converted to private dwellings whilst the Central Junior School built in 1977 is on the Keward Estate. The Secondary Modern School built at Kennion Road in 1955 meant that the school was partly at the Old Priory and partly in the new buildings.

Oakley School pupils (above) in 1934 after the school moved from what is now the Wells Museum. The head teachers were Mr and Mrs Brooks. The school accepted both boys and girls from the age of five; music, dancing and typewriting were offered as special lessons. The school later moved from Priory Road to the Portway. The Wells Museum building was once a Chancellor's House, basically fifteenth century but substantially altered in the eighteenth and nineteenth centuries. In 1880 this house was purchased by Mr Elwes, the Principal of the Theological College and leased from 1881-1926 to the Headmaster of the Cathedral School. In 1928 the Trustees of the College conveyed the house to the Trustees of the Wells Museum and for about five years became the premises of the Oakley School. In 1933 it officially became the Wells Museum with Herbert Balch as curator. He held this post for sixty years; his collection of fossils, minerals and archaeological remains are still housed here.

The people in this photograph are gathered for a Labour demonstration in 1920. Compulsory apprenticeship of pauper children was abolished in 1844. From 1897 regulations stated that children should be over the age of nine, before being employed, and be able to read and write. No child could be bound longer than eight years or over the age of twenty-one. Smithies, cordwainers, butchers, weavers, tuckers, tailors and grocers were the guilds involved in city politics. Other sources of income were derived from the countryside. Cheddar cheese has always been marketed and lead from the Mendips only gave out in the nineteenth century In 1833 the market for cheese was the greatest in the west of England, and one large stocking factory still employed 150 persons. Mendip's clean water has provided a good source for paper making; the famous mills at Wookey Hole and Haybridge can trace their origins back to before the seventeenth century. Longstanding firms had to adapt to meet the changing needs of the modern world.

remained here for sixty-five years In 1986 they moved to No. 38 Market street. After the Second World War thirty staff were employed but the introduction of VAT in the 1970s led to a reduction in the workforce. Paul's employees possessed a wide variety of skills which was considered unusual when rival firms were becoming more specialised. They continued to produce their own paints and to offer high-quality traditional workmanship. The recent photograph shows sons Jack and George Paul who both live within a radius of Wells.

W.H. Paul builders, decorators, glaziers and sign-writers was established in 1893 by William Paul, whose son Harry Paul is seen in the old photograph from around 1920. William had four sons who were all involved in the firm which continued until 1990. Pauls' high quality building work and decoration is still visible around the city today. The business was first set up in South Street. In 1918 the family moved to No. 2 St Cuthbert Street from where the business continued; the builder's yard was situated in Mill Street. They

Crease's was one of the city's leading grocers and provision merchants, situated at Nos 78 and 80 High Street, near St Cuthbert's church. The business was started by Edwin Crease, a native of Westbury-sub-Mendip, in around 1883. Many present-day Wells residents will recall the personal service, glass-topped biscuit tins, delicatessen counter and home deliveries. Pressure from supermarkets and changed shopping and trading patterns led to the closure of the business in the early 1970s. The old photograph, provided by Roger Cookman, Edwin Crease's grandson, shows Edwin Crease outside the shop premises in the early 1900s. Roger recalls, 'Grandfather was one of the first subscribers when the telephone service arrived in Wells in 1906, and had the

number, Wells 4.' Edwin Crease was active in the civic life of the city, being first elected as a councillor in 1907, and retiring as an alderman in 1945. He was mayor on three occasions in the mid-1920s.

The Somerset County Record Office holds data of the first registration of motor vehicles in the county. It is therefore known that this 20hp delivery van, registration number Y3707, was first registered by Edwin Crease on 8 September 1915. The vehicle was based on the famous Ford Model T chassis, and the basic cost at that time would have been approximately £115. The unladen weight is stated to have been about 14 cwt. Sign-writing was carried out separately to individual requirements. The proud driver in his smart livery has been identified as Mr Lane. The recent photograph was taken from outside No. 78, Wells Motor Parts, looking across the road. This delivery lorry is considerably smaller than most such vehicles today.

Maurice Whiting and Mr Wyatt stand in the doorway of No. 68 High Street, around 1936. Whitings was established by John Aubrey Whiting in 1936. Before he opened this shop he was manager of Barnes and Son at No. 41 High Street. When this store closed and Mr Barnes retired, Mr Richards his partner, acquired the plumbing side of the business whilst the general iron mongery, radio and electrical department transferred to No. 68. Here the general public could bring their radio accumulators in to be charged. Whitings were also the official Hoover and Raleigh bicycle agents. Maurice Whiting, the son in Whiting and Son, worked for the firm until he joined the RAF; he was later killed in action. After World War Two and on her father's death Audrey Whiting took over the business. The shop is now run by Michelle Machine her daughter.

The store provides the kind of traditional service rarely found these days. The recent photograph shows todays employees from left to right. Mr M. Seward, Miss E. Thorne, Mrs M. Bowring, Mrs M. Machine, Mr A. Mitchell, Mrs S. Short, Mrs P. Brown, Mr D. Rudd.

Trudgian's Confectioners as they were around 1914 at No. 2 Broad Street. Mr and Mrs Trudgian are seen here with soldiers who were billeted in Broad Street during the First World War. William Trudgian opened a bootmakers shop at No. 1 Mill Lane in 1880. Two years later his wife Matilda took over the running of the business which had by this time moved to No. 3 Broad Street. In 1910 Herbert Samuel, the youngest of her six children set up a confectioners across the road. The shop was enlarged, incorporating additional rooms at street level previously used by the family who lived, as was common practice, above the shop. Jack and Margaret Irene Beer (*née* Trudgian) carried on this business which became known to the locals as Beers. Microbitz now trades from these premises.

Worlds' Stores, a grocers shop seen in the old photograph at No. 12 High Street around 1927, was the forerunner to the supermarkets as we know them today. It was the first multiple pre-supermarket in Wells. Today Tesco, built and opened in 1991, allows the shopper to purchase a range of goods all under one roof, with the added convenience of parking facilities. They began to operate their 'Open all hours' scheme in the summer of 2000. For 24 hours a day, six days a week the store is open. The new arrangement gives people the chance to visit the store in a more leisurely fashion. In contrast, Spencers at No. 4 Tucker Street is a traditional provision merchants. This family business established in 1935 retains many

of the original Victorian fixtures together with a personal counter service. Take a step back to savour the smell of home cooked ham, locally produced cheeses and freshly baked bread.

Previously they had lived at No. 10 across the road where Patrick Hopton's mother Georgina Stevens was born in 1898. Frank converted a former grocer's shop into a garage for his two cars. He was a kind and generous man; on ocassions both he and his wife were known to persuade a reluctant fare-paying passenger into taking along a free rider. Mr Cardwell died in 1979 leaving his property to his brother Jim. Patrick Hopton purchased No. 1 Queen Street in 1984. Milton's Bakery and Griggs Newsagents currently trade from Nos 8 and 10 Queen Street.

Eric Stevens, Frank Cardwell and Jim Cardwell are standing outside No. 8 Queen Street in the old photograph from around 1920. Frank Cardwell and his wife Gwen ran the only taxi service in Wells from the 1930s until the 1970s at which time there were probably a number of other rival firms. In 1932 Cardwell's operated from Nos 3 and 8 Queen Street, advertising themselves as being available 'Anytime anywhere, Cardwell for comfortable cars'. In 1932 Frank purchased No. 1 (the City Arms side) where Kath and Harry Hawkins had been sitting tenants since 1910.

As the early photograph suggests, The China and Glass Shop now at No. 17 Sadler Street was previously known as the Mitre Hotel, one of many hostelries at the turn of the nineteenth century. John and Celia Shepherd have been running the present business for twenty years. It was previously an antique shop run by Ken Taylor who sold the business on to Bernard House in 1973. As far back as 1953 the building was bought by Peter Parrott from previous owners Wicks and Son who now trade at No. 23 Market Place. The china and glass departments have recently amalgamated with 'the Wedding Suite' and now, together, offer a complete wedding list service. Elaine provides exclusive and personally designed bridal gowns and a range of accessories including tiaras, necklaces and shoes. To complete the wedding picture a 1930s Lagonda with driver is also available.

This is the Anchor Public House at No. 13 Market Place, one of the twelve medieval buildings to the north of the Market Place. It is seen in the old photograph being renovated in the 1950s by the firm of W.H. Paul. Access to work at high levels was a problem especially in the early years. Scaffolding was made of wooden poles; these were placed in barrels filled with stone and dust chippings. The cross-members would be lashed onto the verticals with wire ties and was a skilled and time-consuming job. The pub later became the Anchor Restaurant under the management of George Wilkins. Today it is Bernard G. House's Antique Clocks and Scientific Instruments. Mr House first moved to Wells from the north in the early 1970s, having worked for the Imperial Tobacco Company. He originally ran Mitre Antiques in Sadler Street.

When Mr Clare first arrived in Wells from Norfolk in 1900 he opened a drapers shop at No. 4 High Street. He later entered into a partnership with John Henry Holloway the owner of a large general store on the north side of the Market Place. Five years later Clare was the sole owner. Clares originally operated a series of firms established to supply specialised goods to the local dairy industry. The business rapidly expanded taking over several local firms including Hilliers Brush Factory in 1927. Over the last fifty years divisions of the company have gradually been sold off. Clares Engineering Ltd was sold to White, Child and Beney Ltd in 1970 and Clares Carlton was sold to camping suppliers Blacks in 1974. Today Clares MHE Ltd is the only firm left trading under the name

of Clares. Based on the Parkwood Estate they manufacture wirework products, major items being the roll pallets and supermarket trolleys which they supply to all the major supermarket chains in the UK and Europe. The company currently employs 350 staff.

Cecil Dodd and Wilf Paul (above) in 1960, both joined *The Wells Journal* after leaving school at the age of fifteen and retired after serving for fifty years. Alan Tyler in the foreground served his five-year apprenticeship then left to join the RAF. The recent photograph shows *The Wells Journal* staff outside their recently refurbished premises in Southover. Clare Son and Co. Ltd, established in 1851, was yet another of the businesses controlled by Clares. *The Wells Journal* once occupied the Town Hall buildings and was bought by A.J. Clare in 1921. The paper expanded rapidly after the war taking in the *Central Somerset Gazette* in 1945, the *Shepton Mallet Journal* in 1949 and the *Cheddar Valley Gazette* in 1954, thus forming the Mid-Somerset Series. The business was finally sold to the British Printing Corporation in 1964 when the Clare family ceased to have any further connections. A.J. Clare died in 1949 and will be remembered for his pioneering work and prodigious activities not only in his businesses but in and for the local community.

The history of the Sheldon business began in 1880. Alfred Sheldon a local millwright set up his business in West Street, trading as Alfred Sheldon and Sons Ltd. By 1930 the mill had two departments; milling and engineering. The latter was known as Sheldon's Engineering and the milling side of the enterprise has only recently ceased trading. The Bookbarn trades from the former foundry premises. It is the West Country's largest second-hand bookshop with over 140,000 books sold on a percentage commission basis. The shop is open seven days a week throughout the year with more than 2,500 books added each week. James Stratton is seen here serving a customer in the recent photograph. Proposals have been put forward by Kings Oak South West Ltd, for seventy houses to be built on the former Sheldon Milling site facing Strawberry Way.

and Jones Ltd motor engineers at No. 20 High Street and later Gunnings also in Priory Road (Homechime site) who offered Austin sales and services and more recently the Provincial in New Street, now demolished. Presently trading are Webbs in Southover, the Wells Tyre Service Ltd in Webbs Close and Autospeed seen in the recent photograph. This and the SWEB site were previously used by Willmott Transport who relocated in 1981. They ran their Willmott business from here from 1930 having previously operated from the lower end of Portway and later from No. 25 St Cuthbert Street. The company was nationalised in the 1950s during which time Mr Willmott purchased the old Fruit Market from where he ran a coaching service. He later sold this business but retained the lorries on the Autospeed site.

C.T. Jewell's garage is seen in the old photograph at Priory Road, around 1920. This charabanc registration number Y5722 is the same vehicle seen waiting outside the Railway Tavern in Southover (see p. 35). The garage was situated next to the Old Palace Theatre. The city has ben served well by firms such as Sampson

William and Emily Mogg arrived in Wells in the mid-nineteenth century from Kings Stag on the Somerset, Dorset border. They initially ran a bakery at No. 7 Southover, later moving to No. 52 High Street where the Jersey Dairy and Restaurant were added. The Moggs had nine children. Son Sidney carried on the family business in th High Street, whilst the youngest child, William Bertram became an apprentice to John Knight at No. 3 High Street. In 1905 Bertram set up his own business at No. 6 Sadler Street. In the 1920s when son Bert joined the firm the freehold of No. 5 Sadler Street was purchased. For a short time business traded on both sides of Sadler Street. Bertram purchased Cherry Orchard in 1918, which was a farm at this time taking in land down to the Wookey Hole Road. Additional fields at Fir Tor Avenue, Orchard Lea and Goodymoor were also rented. Moggs were producers of

agricultural machinery, milking machines and dairy equipment during the 1950s and 1960s. The business now sells horticultural and gardening equipment. Bert's son Basil took over the business in 1972. The recent photograph shows, from left to right: Nigel Barnes, Diana Ford, Sue Jackman, Peter Roper, Basil Mogg, Ashley Hodges, Michael Hayter, Michael Dampler.

As Browne and Sons (after a name change) and later as W.J. Browne, seedsman and florist, they supplied everything from agricultural seeds to subtropical plants. The seeds were an important branch of the business. Pasture and other grasses were also available as well as lawn grass seed, white Dutch clover and ornamental grasses. Asparagus was 7s 6d and seakale 12s per 100 and there were sundry bulbs and roots for spring planting. Lawnmowers, garden rollers and garden implements could be purchased. In 1973 the Priory Nurseries and orchard were sold. The business relocated to its present site on the outskirts of Wells on the Glastonbury Road. The recent photograph shows Jonathan Browne with his wife and son George.

Emmanuel Brown established Brown's Nursery in New Street in 1808. This business may well be the oldest surviving family enterprise in Wells. It has seen eight generations over the last 200 years. In 1901 they were trading from a branch at No. 31. Sadler Street and new premises at No. 2 Princes Road as the Priory Nursery. Walter Emmanuel, son of Emmanuel Brown, was born in 1835. He is seen here in the old photograph in one of the orchards attached to the nursery.

On 11 July 1913 Mr Hucks visited Wells after being invited by the Amateur Athletic Union to put on a flying demonstration to encourage visitors to the city. This two-day event was held at the Athletic Ground. At 4 p.m. on the first day Mr Hucks took off. He proceeded around Glastonbury and Butleigh, encircling the Tor, and then returned to Wells. Later that same day he flew over Dulcote and Shepton Mallet at a height of 3,000 feet. He returned to Wells from an easterly direction and to the surprise and wonder of those in the vicinity, he dropped down over the roof of the nave of the Cathedral, cleverly piloting his machine between the north and south towers. The event attracted a total of 3,500 locals and visitors. Andy Elson,

Chapter 5
LEISURE AND
ENTERTAINMENT

the balloonist who designed and flew the balloon that circumnavigated the world in 1999, lives in Wells. He also developed the special burners needed to operate balloons flying above 30,000ft, thus enabling him to fly the first balloon over Mount Everest in 1991.

THOMAS' GARDEN FÊTE
WELLS

376

Youngsters are seen here providing entertainment at the St Thomas Garden Fête in 1915. The first May Day Festival, sponsored by the Wells Lions held in the market place raised hundreds of pounds for city charities and provided an unexpected treat for Bank Holiday visitors. The Wells Lions wanted to revive the spirit of the May-time once a part of country life centuries ago. The Maypole used was donated by Eddie Nowell, Antique dealer. The Maypole cup also donated by Mr Nowell is now awarded in a Maypole Dance Competition amongst local schools.

The old photograph shows the Crown Hotel Carnival entry in 1929. From left to right are: Barbara (seated) and Audrey Price, Sidney and Cyril Price, Cherry Hawes and Gordon Hawes (seated far left). In 1902 there were twenty-six floats to celebrate Coronation Day. By 1932 mechanical haulage resulted in a steady increase in the size of floats. At this time the procession not only toured the historic centre but visited the Cottage Hospital via the Liberty, North Road and St Thomas Street. It barely turned the North Road corner just as modern floats have trouble with the corner of High Street and Sadler Street today. Most floats now come from organisations and specialist clubs.

Members work for months and large sums are spent on materials. The results are seen over a period of about two weeks in November during the carnival circuit of Somerset towns.

The roads surrounding the area were closed whilst emergency forces were called in. The second mishap involved the Carnival Queen's royal float which was involved in an accident. The float became uncoupled from its towing tractor and crashed into a car. Last, but not least, the heavens opened and the weather became the third calamity. A large number of the crowd left early but for hardy carnivalites who defied the weather, it was still the magical combination of light and sound. The monster floats with their giant casts and thousands of glittering bulbs generated the same enthusiasm as the drenched but defiant single walking entries and the smaller clubs struggling to keep spluttering generators working. In the end calamity was defied and as always, the show went on.

Harry Paul as Sir Francis Drake seen here in 1902 received second prize in the carnival competition. The 2000 millennium carnival celebrations were not without a fair share of misfortune. The first catastrophe struck before the wheels of the first float had turned and the carnival was threatened by a massive explosion, and came within an hour of being cancelled altogether. A gas leak at the Regal Cinema corner was discovered where repairs to a conduit had been underway for some weeks.

The Chorus from a production of *The Merry Widow* in 1963 are wearing their Pontevedrian costumes in the old photograph. The recent picture captures a moment during the production of *Me and My Girl*, in spring 2000. In 1902 the Wells Operatic Society was formed. Their home at this time was the Town Hall. The Byre Theatre, a long single-storey building at the lower end of Chamberlain Street, was used for productions of more serious nature and the Wells Theatre formerly a non-conformist chapel with St Cuthberts Rooms was situated at the end of Priest Row, opposite the Globe. Lantern slide shows were held here and it also served as a refuge for evacuees during the war. In 1968 the city council offered the Operatic Society the Old Blue School premises.

The theatre was eventually purchased in 1979. The building was gradually modified and now has seating for 170. The normal yearly programme consists of a Christmas pantomime, a large musical production in the spring and a smaller light musical in the autumn.

Wells was once graced with two excellent cinemas; the Regal and Palace Theatre both in Priory Road. The Palace Theatre seen to the far left, around 1920, was originally a bottling factory later converted to a theatre, and then in the 1930s to a cinema. It was never quite able to compete with the Regal built in 1935. It was last used as a cinema in the 1960s and was run by Edward Collins. In 1998 the theatre was demolished and another historical landmark was lost. The Regal Cinema continued to be used up to more recent times; however, it now stands empty and has been subjected to much vandalisation. An urgent works notice has been served on the owners requiring them to carry out necessary repairs to preserve the fabric of this listed building which is considered to be an outstanding example of Art Deco design. It was first listed in 1991 after which the owners applied for permission to develop it into a leisure complex with a studio, cinema, restaurant and disco. At the time the Cinema Theatre Association raised strong objections, considering the destructive and irreversible nature of any conversions.

Elizabeth Goudge dubbed her birthplace 'A City of Bells'. Today the bells from St Thomas, St Cuthbert and the Cathedral all sound the hour, and every quarter in the case of the latter. In the Middle Ages the Priory of St John was said to have the right to ring bells, and in the sixteenth and seventeenth centuries there was a bell on the top of the conduit which had to be rung before any market trading was permitted. The Cathedral has the world's heaviest ring of ten bells. Three new bells, the first to be installed in Wells Cathedral for more than 100 years, were recently blessed. They weigh 14cwt, 7cwt and 4cwt and are called Faith, Hope and Love. The two larger bells will be rung for services and the third will ring the *Angelus* each day at noon. They have been given to the Cathedral in memory of three Banwell families

Cathedral bell is re-hung.

who had strong connections with church campanology. These photographs show the re-hanging of the Cathedral bell, and bellringers at St Cuthberts who meet every Friday between 7.30 p.m. and 9 p.m.

Mayor Maureen Brandon judged the entries at the East Somerset Railway, Cranmore; cream teas and the prize giving were held in the Town Hall. The Best Dressed Male award went to Richard Leworthy and the Best Dressed Lady was Mr Atkinson's partner. Among other awards were Best Pre and Post-war cars, Most Desirable car and Best Classic car. The club was formed by a group of enthusiasts in 1976 to cater for all cars manufactured before 1 January 1959. This was changed in 1995 to a thirty year rolling date from date of first registration. The aims are to encourage the use and preservation of old motor cars. The main competitive events fall between April and October. Club life continues in the winter with a Sunday lunch once a month and members receive a monthly magazine, *Classix*.

The Market Place is seen in the old photograph in around 1920. The Classic and Historic Motor Club held their fifth Mendip Vintage and Classic Tour on 14 May 2000. The cars left Victoria Park in Bath and finished on the Cathedral Green at 3. 30 p.m.

Former mayor Jack Munden and Tony Williams weigh out the money collected for the Boys' Club built in Princes Road next to the old fire station. Onlookers include, to the far right, Kevin White. In 1950 a boxing tournament was held at the Mendip Hospital. As a result of its success a boxing club was formed and ultimately funds were raised to provide for the club. The building was converted in 1992 into the Wells Film Centre and is run by Derek Cooper and his family who previously ran a video-hire shop in St Cuthbert Street. They have recently celebrated their eighth year and plans to improve the front of the building, move

the entrance to the side and offer better box office facilities and provide a licensed bar for customers are proposed to take place in the near future.

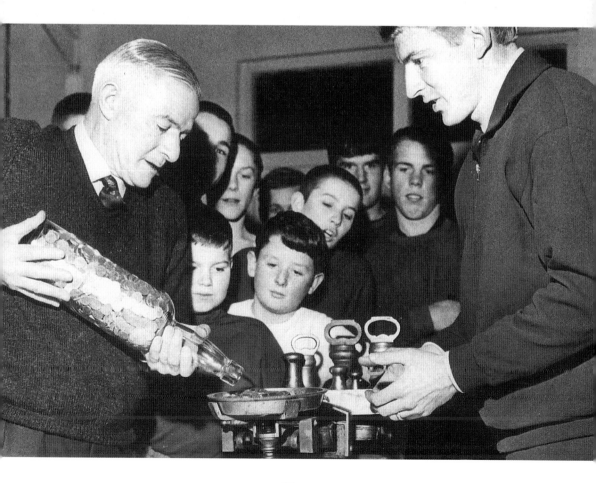

Army Cadets are lined up in front of the TA lorry in 1953 before leaving for their annual camp. Both Army and Air Cadets still meet for regular training on the MOD site in Webbs Close. The recent photograph of the Air Training Corps was taken on 20 July 2000 at their annual open evening. The commanding Officer is Flight Lieutenant John Heath. The RAF supply the uniforms and equip and maintain the buildings. The cadets get a chance to gain flying experience and go on camps across the country as well as abroad to Gibraltar, Cyprus and Germany. Four cadets achieved their Duke of Edinburgh Gold Awards in 2000. Meetings are held every Monday and Thursday evenings.

The 'Salute the Soldier Ceremony' was held on 18 June 1944; the ceremony was one of the many events put on to raise funds for the war effort. Since this time the Cathedral Green has been used to stage various events and concerts to raise funds. Profits from this year's music on the Green went to the Wookey Hole branch of Riding for the Disabled. Concerts held here have hosted major star performers such as Rolf Harris and Cleo Lane. The annual Somerset Schools Folk Dance Festival held in June is another spectacular event which has probably become the largest gathering of primary schools in the country with eighty-five participating schools. The day begins at 2 p.m. when the children form a colourful procession up the

High Street from St Cuthbert's church, led by the mayor and other civic dignitaries. This year saw its twenty-fifth anniversary which was masterminded by Harvey Siggs, head of Wells Community education.

The top photograph from 1950 shows former Mayor Kippax at the end of season swimming club presentations, held at the Corporation swimming pool in Princes Road. This pool, together with the old fire station

was demolished to provide space for the new Tesco supermarket built in 1991. Wells' first swimming pool was in Ash Lane and was leased to the Corporation. In 1955 the pool in Princes Road with its outdoor heated 100ft x 35ft pool and sun-bathing terraces was considered to be one of the finest and most up-to-date in the West of England. Local schools and the Swimming Club had regular weekly sessions throughout the summer months. It was open daily from May to September. A children's paddling pool was a later addition. 1991 saw the opening of the new leisure centre with its 25m indoor heated pool, health suite, additional sports facilities and poolside cafeteria. The recent photograph shows the jacuzzi in the foreground with the main pool to the far left and small pool to the right.

Wells Bowling Club was first set up in 1910 at the Athletic Ground. Eventually in 1914 the club moved to the Recreation Ground. where it remains today. The green is said to be one of the truest and best laid in the county. Bowls was a game played mainly by the gentry, businessmen, city archaeologists and engineers, as for most of the working population there was not much leisure time. There were discussions, during the war, for this area to be turned into allotments; strong opposition prevailed. Women were finally admitted in the 1930s. The 2000 season was launched on Saturday 14 April when the most senior member George Smith bowled the opening bowl in conditions more suited to winter sports. On 23 May 2000 a

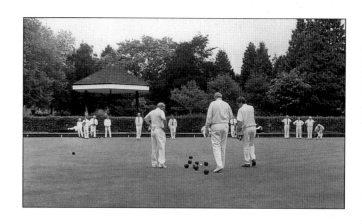

friendly match was played against Pembroke as seen in the recent photograph. The start of the game was delayed in the hope that rain would stop. After playing in atrocious weather the game was adjourned for refreshments.

The top photograph shows the Wells Wednesday cricket team, made up mostly of local farmers and businessmen, in around 1960. Back row from left to right: Frank Treasure (umpire), Rob Crocker, Reg Tinknell, Mike Wilson, George Vowles, Eric Purchase, John Sealy, Ted Trafford (umpire). Front row from left to right: Roger Raywood, Mike Underdown, Gordon Collins, Bill Brown, Les Moore (president). The Wells City Cricket Club was founded in 1921. The team members called themselves the 'stragglers'. With money raised they bought a couple of bats, borrowed kit and played a few matches. The First XI proved so successful that they decided to form a club. To score with any success at this time it was necessary to hit hard and high with the hope that the ball would be lost in the long grass giving the fielders a long hunt. In 1927 the club became affiliated to the Somerset County Cricket Club; by this time they had become well established and financially sound. The recent photograph shows the Wells County Cricket team playing on their pitch in front of the old Mendip Hospital.

The Mendip Rugby Football Club was established in 1876. The bottom photograph shows players from 1952; there are a number of famous faces here, who at one time played for the club. They are: Alec Lewis who was the only international player to win ten caps for England between 1952 and 1954; the late Keith Showering, who later became Sir Keith of Babycham fame; and Noel Jones, a student at the Theological College who later became Bishop of Sodor and Man. In 1972 the club was renamed the Wells Rugby Football Club. The recent picture was taken at the Portway ground prior to the opening match of the season against Imperial; they scored a 43-11 win. The club begins pre-season training in July with a players'

meeting in the club house after the mid-week training session. A colts XV is now open to any player aged sixteen to nineteen years. The Bristol and District Colts League which came into being in 1999 has proved extremely popular with teams in the area.

The Wells City Football Club was founded in 1890. Their first pitch was at Torfurlong, then named Torfairlands. They moved to the athletic ground in 1894. Pictured here are members of the club in 1922. They won the Somerset Senior league three times in the first four years, progressing to the Western league. In 1948 as one of the oldest amateur clubs in the country they decided to turn professional. This led to the legendary Ernie Jones joining after being released by Bristol City. Under his inspiration and for the first time in the club's history they won the title in 1950. In 1957 they reverted to amateur status, returning to the Somerset Senior league after sixty-four years of absence. In the '70s, Wells continued to enjoy success. Eddie Westmoreland, who achieved league success with Carlise United, joined the Wells Club and with his influence they became runners-up in the 1973 Somerset Senior League. Richard Sheard took over as chairman in 1995, since which time the club has become a force to be reckoned with.

In 1964 Mary Rand, known as Wells' 'golden girl' and pictured here in 1960, achieved a world record in the ladies' long jump at the Olympic Games in Tokyo. She was also the first British woman Olympic gold medallist. A plaque and a gateway to the athletic ground commemorates and honours her outstanding successes which was a magnificent jump of 22ft 2in. The length of her jump is measured out in brass on the market place pavement in front of the Bekynton's Brasserie. At the same games she also won a silver medal and thus brought fame to her native city, her county and her country. In keeping with tradition and with other well-known citizens, Bignal Rand Drive and Mary Road are named after her. Wells' 'golden girl' is seen jumping in front of a home crowed at the

WELLS' GOLDEN GIRL.

recreation ground. A suggestion has been made recently for the gateway (left) to be moved to a more prominent position where it can be better seen by both residents and visitors.

welcomed by the Mayor John Howett, the chairman of Mendip District Council and the former head of BBC Sport, Cliff Morgan. Winners of the afternoon's events were presented with their awards and Mary's plaque marking the record breaking jump was rededicated. Lynn Davies was the first British man to win an Olympic field event title. He also won the men's long jump in the Tokyo Olympic Games. Ann Packer started her career as a sprinter, hurdler and jumper. In Tokyo at the age of twenty-two she broke the world record and won the gold medal in the 800 metres; she went on to win a silver in the 400 metres. Mary Peters won a gold in the Pentathlon at the 1972 Munich games.

Penniless Porch and The Bekynton Café are seen from around 1932 in the old photograph. In July 1994 Mary Bignal Rand returned as a star guest at a weekend of athletics celebrations held in the city. The festivities began at noon with the Wells City Band followed by a pole vault competition in the market place. In the afternoon amid cheers Mary made her entrance. Three other British gold medallists, Lynn Davies, Ann Packer and Mary Peters, were also

Mark Cross, alias Arthur Valentine gives a much needed polish to the brass plaque outside No. 3 High Street. It commemorates the second gift of running water in the city given by Richard Lord Bishop of Bath and Wells in 1803. Mark Cross lived in the Vicars Close and wrote thrillers and the song *Three o'clock in the Morning*. He was father to the well-known cuisinier Fanny Craddock. The old conduit built in 1451 was a large, four-square building designed to harmonise with the old cross which stood a little to the east between the conduit and the Exchequer in the centre of the market place. Water ran in lead pipes 12 inches in circumference from a conduit in the grounds of the Bishop's Palace to the Market Place. In 1797 the medieval conduit was replaced by the Gothic creation which we see today. At one time there were two public conduits; that in the market place and the other at the top of Broad Street near Mill Street. Two wardens were responsible for the repair and management of both these conduits.

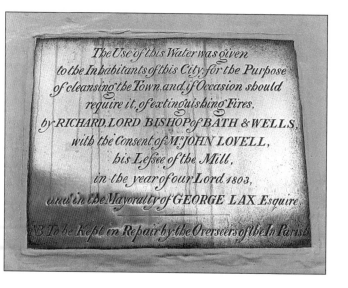

Wells but returned home early. The next day he accompanied the mayor and city council to St Cuthberts for the Remembrance Day Service. As a tribute to this much liked and respected figure, the Union Jack was flown at half mast from the Town Hall. Fred Gibbons, his predecessor, who held the post for fifteen years and was considered to be the 'Voice of Wells' appearing in many tourism films, has also died recently. He was made a life member of the Ancient and Honourable Guild of Town Criers Wells in March 2000. On 7 September 2001 Wells celebrates 800 years of its Royal Charter originally signed by King John in 1201.

The old photograph shows St Cuthbert's church fête in July 1958. From left to right are Cllr Mogg, Mrs Mogg, Town Crier Jack Davies and Preb Barnett. The modern picture shows town cryer Les Long who died suddenly on 15 November 2000 at the age of sixty-nine. Mr Long was a printer with *The Wells Journal* until he retired. For many years he was chairman of the city's carnival committee and was later its president. He was also a highly respected judge on the carnival circuit. He attended the Millennium event in